INSPIRAT

Fathers

ecpa Member of the Evangelical Christian Publishers Association

INSPIRATION FOR
Fathers

BARBOUR
PUBLISHING

Choose you this day whom ye will serve. . .as for me
and my house, we will serve the LORD.

JOSHUA 24:15

Bless your children and you bless your future.

CONOVER SWOFFORD

I cannot think of any need in childhood
as strong as the need for a father's protection.

SIGMUND FREUD

Do not handicap your children
by making their lives easy.

ROBERT A. HEINLEIN

Give a little love to a child,
and you get a great deal back.

JOHN RUSKIN

Years from now, they'll remember you by what they see in your kids.

BILL BUTTERWORTH

The most valuable contribution a parent can make to a child is to instill in him or her a genuine faith in Jesus Christ.

JAMES DOBSON

These words, which I command thee this day, shall be in thine heart: and thou shalt teach them diligently unto thy children, and shalt talk of them when thou sittest in thine house, and when thou walkest by the way, and when thou liest down, and when thou risest up.

Deuteronomy 6:6–7

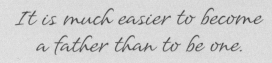

It is much easier to become
a father than to be one.

KENT NERBURN

The difficult thing about children
is that they come with no instructions.
You pretty well have to assemble them on your own.

JAMES DOBSON

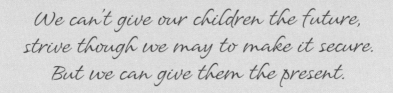

*We can't give our children the future,
strive though we may to make it secure.
But we can give them the present.*

KATHLEEN NORRIS

Sometimes the poorest man leaves his children the richest inheritance.

RUTH E. RENKEL

The voice of parents is the voice of God's,
for to their children, they are heaven's lieutenants.

WILLIAM SHAKESPEARE

Train up a child in the way he should go:
and when he is old, he will not depart from it.

PROVERBS 22:6

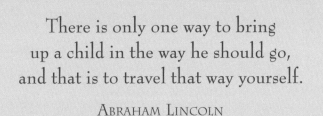

There is only one way to bring
up a child in the way he should go,
and that is to travel that way yourself.

ABRAHAM LINCOLN

If you must hold yourself up to
your children as an object lesson,
hold yourself up as a warning
and not as an example.

GEORGE BERNARD SHAW

Noble fathers have noble children.

EURIPIDES

Children are natural mimics who act
like their parents despite every effort
to teach them good manners.

UNKNOWN

It is easier for a father to have children than for children to have a real father.

POPE JOHN XXIII

In the final analysis it is not what you do
for your children but what you have taught them
to do for themselves that will make them
successful human beings.

ANN LANDERS

Nothing you do for children is ever wasted.
They seem not to notice us, hovering,
averting our eyes; and they seldom offer thanks,
but what we do for them is never wasted.

GARRISON KEILLOR

Don't worry that children never listen to you;
worry that they are always watching you.

ROBERT FULGHUM

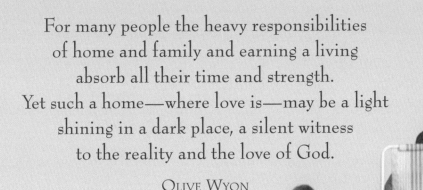

For many people the heavy responsibilities
of home and family and earning a living
absorb all their time and strength.
Yet such a home—where love is—may be a light
shining in a dark place, a silent witness
to the reality and the love of God.

OLIVE WYON

Happiness is to be found only in the home where
God is loved and honored, where each one loves,
and helps, and cares for the others.

<small>THEOPHANES VENARD</small>

*Let parents bequeath to their children not riches,
but the spirit of reverence.*

PLATO

The simple exercise of praying together regularly as a family will do more to strengthen your family than anything else you could do together.

BRUCE BICKEL AND STAN JANTZ

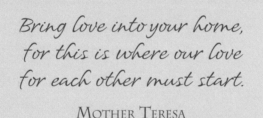

*Bring love into your home,
for this is where our love
for each other must start.*

MOTHER TERESA

Sacred and happy homes
are the surest guarantees
for the moral progress of a nation.

HENRY DRUMMOND

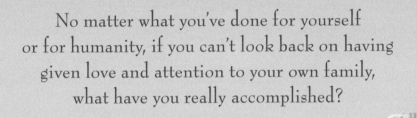

No matter what you've done for yourself
or for humanity, if you can't look back on having
given love and attention to your own family,
what have you really accomplished?

Lee Iacocca

The family is the nucleus of civilization.

WILLIAM J. DURANT

Every Christian family ought to be, as it were,
a little church consecrated to Christ
and wholly influenced and governed by His rules.

JONATHAN EDWARDS

We can't form our children on our own concepts;
we must take them and love them
as God gives them to us.

JOHANN WOLFGANG VON GOETHE

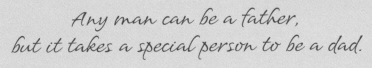

Any man can be a father,
but it takes a special person to be a dad.

ANONYMOUS

Life affords no greater responsibility, no greater privilege, than the raising of the next generation.

C. EVERETT KOOP

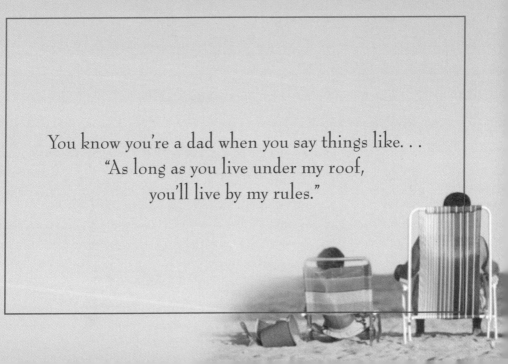

You know you're a dad when you say things like. . .
"As long as you live under my roof,
you'll live by my rules."

You know you're a dad when you say things like. . .
"I'm not just talking to hear my own voice!"

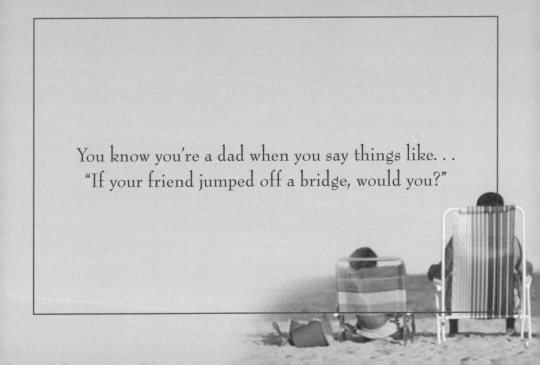

You know you're a dad when you say things like. . .
"If your friend jumped off a bridge, would you?"

You know you're a dad when you say things like. . .
"In my day. . ."

You know you're a dad when you say things like. . .
"Don't ask me; ask your mother."

You know you're a dad when you say things like. . .
"A little dirt never hurt anyone. . . . Just wipe it off."

You know you're a dad when you say things like...
"I told you...keep your eye on the ball."

You know you're a dad when you say things like. . .
"We're not lost. I'm just not sure where we are."

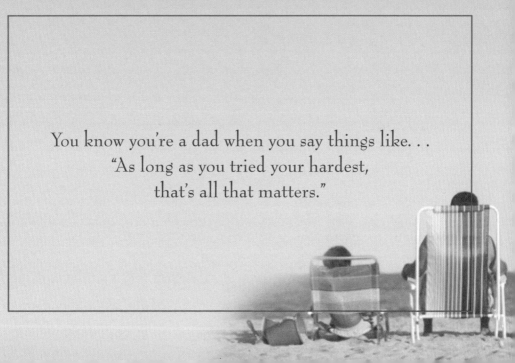

You know you're a dad when you say things like. . .
"As long as you tried your hardest,
that's all that matters."

Lo, children are an heritage of the LORD.

Psalm 127:3

Blessed indeed is the man who hears
many gentle voices call him Father!

LYDIA M. CHILD

As arrows are in the hand of a mighty man;
so are children of the youth.
Happy is the man that hath his quiver full of them.

Psalm 127:4–5

There are only two things
we should give our children.
One is roots; the other, wings.

HODDING CARTER

*There is no friendship, no love,
like that of the parent for the child.*

HENRY WARD BEECHER

Until you have a son of your own. . .you will never know the joy, the love beyond feeling that resonates in the heart of a father as he looks upon his son. You will never know the sense of honor that makes a man want to be more than he is and to pass something good and hopeful into the hands of his son.

KENT NERBURN

To a father growing old,
nothing is dearer than a daughter.

EURIPIDES

Tribute to Dad

F. . . You are my friend.
A. . . You are my ally.
T. . . You are my teacher.
H. . . You are my hero.
E. . . You are my example.
R. . . You are my rock.

There is no more vital calling or vocation for men than fathering.

JOHN THROOP

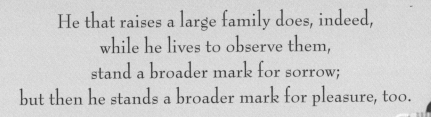

He that raises a large family does, indeed,
while he lives to observe them,
stand a broader mark for sorrow;
but then he stands a broader mark for pleasure, too.

BENJAMIN FRANKLIN

Children are poor men's riches.

ENGLISH PROVERB

My father gave me the greatest gift anyone could give another person—he believed in me.

Jim Valvano

One night a father overheard his son pray:
"Dear God, make me the kind of man my daddy is."
Later that night, the father prayed,
"Dear God, make me the kind of man
my son wants me to be."

ANONYMOUS

The greatest gift I ever had came from God,
and I call him Dad!

ANONYMOUS

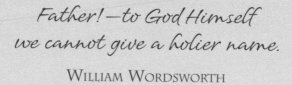

Father!—to God Himself
we cannot give a holier name.

WILLIAM WORDSWORTH

I've had a hard life, but my hardships are nothing against the hardships that my father went through in order to get me to where I started.

BARTRAND HUBBARD

*Every man is rich who has a child
to love and guide.*

OUR DAILY BREAD

I have no greater joy than to hear
that my children walk in truth.

3 JOHN 1:4

He didn't tell me how to live; he lived, and let me watch him do it.

CLARENCE BUDINGTON KELLAND

I love my father as the stars—he's a bright,
shining example and a happy twinkling in my heart.

ADABELLA RADICI

The most important thing a father can do for his children is to love their mother.

DAVID O. MCKAY

Children's children are the crown of old men;
and the glory of children are their fathers.

PROVERBS 17:6

A man's children and his garden both
reflect the amount of weeding done
during the growing season.

UNKNOWN

Kids learn by example. If I respect Mom, they're going to respect Mom.

Tim Allen

*He who teaches children learns
more than they do.*

GERMAN PROVERB

We cannot always build the future for our youth,
but we can build our youth for the future.

FRANKLIN D. ROOSEVELT

During the course of the day,
I frequently ask the Lord to give me wisdom
to use the knowledge that I have
and to give me perspective and understanding,
particularly when difficult situations arise.

BEN CARSON

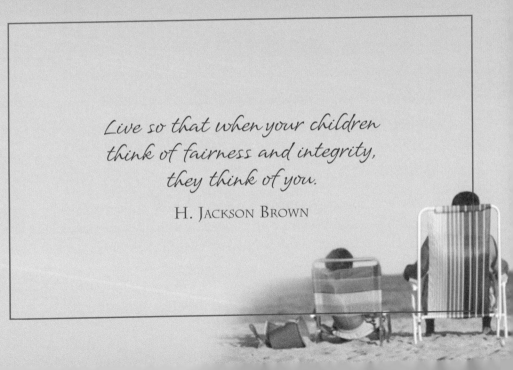

Live so that when your children think of fairness and integrity, they think of you.

H. JACKSON BROWN

None of the things I remember about my father
had anything at all to do with his lifestyle
or whom he knew or the places he had been
or the style of the clothes he wore.
I just knew that he was always there.

CAL THOMAS

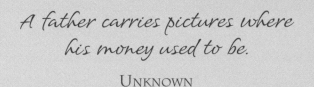

A father carries pictures where his money used to be.

UNKNOWN

Your children need your *presence*
more than your *presents*.

JESSE JACKSON

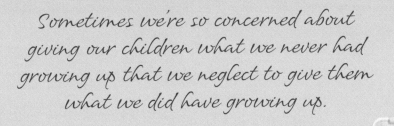

Sometimes we're so concerned about giving our children what we never had growing up that we neglect to give them what we did have growing up.

JAMES DOBSON

When a father gives to his son, both laugh;
when a son gives to his father, both cry.

JEWISH PROVERB

There's nothing that can help you understand your beliefs more than trying to explain them to an inquisitive child.

FRANK A. CLARK

My son, despise not the chastening of the LORD;
neither be weary of his correction:
for whom the LORD loveth he correcteth;
even as a father the son in whom he delighteth.

PROVERBS 3:11–12

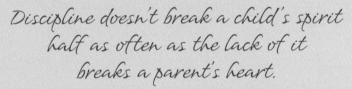

Discipline doesn't break a child's spirit half as often as the lack of it breaks a parent's heart.

ANONYMOUS

*It behooves a father to be blameless
if he expects his child to be.*

HOMER

The guys who fear becoming fathers don't understand
that fathering is not something perfect men do,
but something that perfects the man.
The end product of child-raising
is not the child but the parent.

FRANK PITTMAN

Character is largely caught,
and the father and the home should be
the great sources of character infection.

FRANK H. CHELEY

Children are apt to live up to what you believe of them.

LADY BIRD JOHNSON

The father of the righteous shall greatly rejoice:
and he that begetteth a wise child shall have joy of him.

PROVERBS 23:24

Character may be manifested
in the great moments,
but it is made in the small ones.

PHILLIPS BROOKS

Few things help an individual more
than to place responsibility upon him
and to let him know that you trust him.

BOOKER T. WASHINGTON

It is a wise father that knows his own child.

WILLIAM SHAKESPEARE

The best portion of a good man's life
is his little, nameless, unremembered
acts of kindness and love.

WILLIAM WORDSWORTH

Don't be misled by the myth of
"quality time"—it is an admirable goal,
but it should not be used as an excuse for missing
"quantity time" with your child.
Quality moments usually cannot be scheduled.
They happen spontaneously, without warning,
in circumstances you don't anticipate.

BRUCE BICKEL AND
STAN JANTZ

For where your treasure is,
there will your heart be also.

MATTHEW 6:21

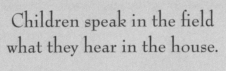

Children speak in the field
what they hear in the house.

SCOTTISH PROVERB

*If you want your children to improve,
let them overhear the nice things
you say about them to others.*

HAIM GINOTT

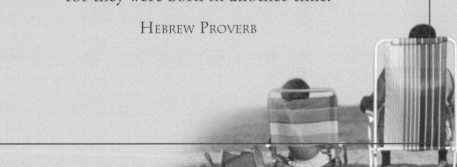

Do not confine your children to your own learning,
for they were born in another time.

HEBREW PROVERB

A truly rich man is one whose children run into his arms when his hands are empty.

UNKNOWN

Don't be discouraged if your
children reject your advice.
Years later they will offer it
to their own offspring.

UNKNOWN

The just man walketh in his integrity:
his children are blessed after him.

PROVERBS 20:7

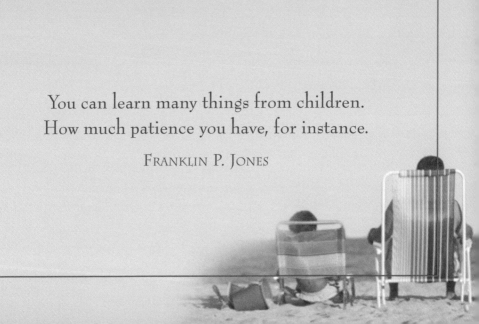

You can learn many things from children.
How much patience you have, for instance.

FRANKLIN P. JONES

Bricks and mortar make a house,
but the laughter of children makes a home.

IRISH PROVERB

*A good father reflects the love
of the heavenly Father.*

UNKNOWN

Let us look upon our children,
let us love them and train them,
as children of the covenant and children
of the promise—these are the children of God.

ANDREW MURRAY

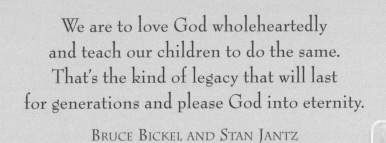

We are to love God wholeheartedly
and teach our children to do the same.
That's the kind of legacy that will last
for generations and please God into eternity.

BRUCE BICKEL AND STAN JANTZ

You have to love your children unselfishly.
That is hard. But it is the only way.

BARBARA BUSH

There are two great injustices that can befall a child.
One is to punish him for something he didn't do.
The other is to let him get away with doing
something he knows is wrong.

ROBERT GARDNER

Even a child is known by his doings,
whether his work be pure, and whether it be right.

PROVERBS 20:11

One father is more than
a hundred schoolmasters.

George Herbert

Our goal is to steadily turn our children away
from their earthly parents, who will let them down,
toward a heavenly Father who will always be there
for them and in whose arms they will always be secure.

<small>Susan Alexander Yates</small>

*Love and fear: Everything the father
of a family says must inspire
one or the other.*

JOSEPH JOUBERT

*That energy which makes a child
hard to manage is the energy which
afterwards makes him a manager of life.*

HENRY WARD BEECHER

By the time a man realizes
that maybe his father was right,
he usually has a son who thinks he's wrong.

CHARLES WADSWORTH

4 years:	My daddy can do anything!
12 years:	Oh well, naturally, Father does not know that either.
18 years:	Oh, that man—he is out-of-date!
25 years:	He knows a little bit about it, but not much.
30 years:	I must find out what Dad thinks about it.
50 years:	What would Dad have thought about that?
65 years:	I wish I could talk it over with Dad once more.

ANONYMOUS

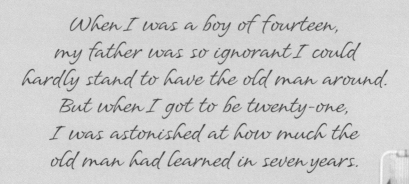

When I was a boy of fourteen,
my father was so ignorant I could
hardly stand to have the old man around.
But when I got to be twenty-one,
I was astonished at how much the
old man had learned in seven years.

MARK TWAIN

Children seldom misquote you.
In fact, they usually repeat word for word
what you shouldn't have said.

UNKNOWN

Children are a great comfort in your old age—
and they help you reach it faster, too.

LIONEL KAUFFMAN

Someday you will know that a father is much happier in his children's happiness than in his own. I cannot explain it to you: It is a feeling in your body that spreads gladness through you.

HONORÉ DE BALZAC

A father is the hands that hold you safe.

UNKNOWN

Can't you see the Creator of the universe,
who understands every secret, every mystery,
sitting patiently and listening
to a four-year-old talk to Him?
That's a beautiful image of a father.

JAMES DOBSON

To show a child what once delighted you,
to find the child's delight added to your own—
this is happiness.

J. B. PRIESTLEY

How many hopes and fears, how many
ardent wishes and anxious apprehensions
are twisted together in the threads
that connect the parent with the child!

SAMUEL G. GOODRICH

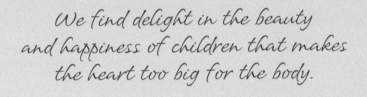

*We find delight in the beauty
and happiness of children that makes
the heart too big for the body.*

RALPH WALDO EMERSON

*We never know the love of our parents
for us till we have become parents ourselves.*

HENRY WARD BEECHER

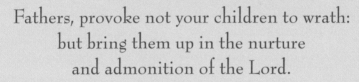

Fathers, provoke not your children to wrath:
but bring them up in the nurture
and admonition of the Lord.

EPHESIANS 6:4

A parent must respect the spiritual person
of his child and approach it with reverence.

GEORGE MACDONALD

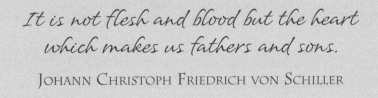

*It is not flesh and blood but the heart
which makes us fathers and sons.*

JOHANN CHRISTOPH FRIEDRICH VON SCHILLER

My dad told me when I went into high school, "It's not what you do when you walk in the door that matters. It's what you do when you walk out." That's when you've made a lasting impression.

JIM THOME

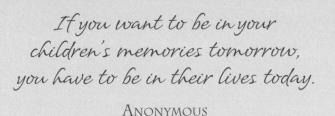

*If you want to be in your
children's memories tomorrow,
you have to be in their lives today.*

ANONYMOUS

We have a suggestion for the perfect gift for your child.
It is not easy to find, and it is terribly expensive,
but we guarantee that it will last a lifetime
and it will be your child's favorite.
We're talking about your *time*.

BRUCE BICKEL AND STAN JANTZ

*Educate your children to self-control,
to the habit of holding passion
and prejudice and evil tendencies subject
to an upright and reasoning will, and you
have done much to abolish misery from
their future and crimes from society.*

BENJAMIN FRANKLIN

If you raise your children to feel that they can
accomplish any goal or task they decide upon,
you will have succeeded as a parent,
and you will have given your children
the greatest of all blessings.

BRIAN TRACY

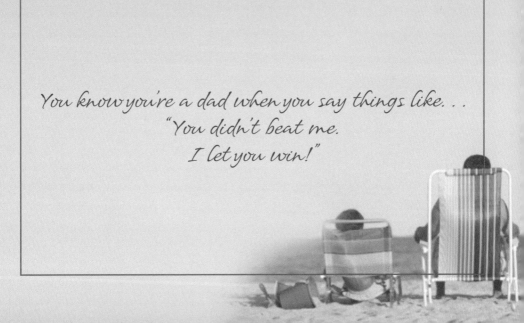

You know you're a dad when you say things like. . .
"You didn't beat me.
I let you win!"

You know you're a dad when you say things like. . .
"No, we're not there yet!"

You know you're a dad when you say things like. . .
"Eat it! It will grow hair on your chest."

You know you're a dad when you say things like. . .
"I'm not sleeping—I was watching
the show on that channel."

You know you're a dad when you say things like. . .
"Turn off those lights.
Do you think I'm made of money?"

Fatherhood is pretending the present you love most is "soap-on-a-rope."

BILL COSBY

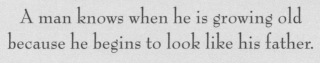

A man knows when he is growing old
because he begins to look like his father.

GABRIEL GARCÍA MÁRQUEZ

All the great blessings of my life are present in my thoughts today.

PHOEBE CARY

When was the last time that you told your children that they are a blessing to you?

CONOVER SWOFFORD

Pray that you may be an example
and a blessing unto others and that you may
live more to the glory of your Master.

CHARLES H. SPURGEON

Being a father is one of the greatest joys
God can give a man.

UNKNOWN

Life is what we are alive to.
It is not length but breadth. . . .
Be alive to. . .goodness, kindness, purity, love,
history, poetry, music, flowers, stars, God,
and eternal hope.

MALTBIE D. BABCOCK

*Fathers, provoke not your children to anger,
lest they be discouraged.*

C<small>OLOSSIANS</small> 3:21

Is there any joy that compares to seeing your newborn child for the first time?

CONOVER SWOFFORD

God is to be seen in the light of a cottage window
as well as in the sun or the stars.

ARTHUR G. CLUTTON-BROCK

*Nothing is more rewarding than
to see the look on a happy child's face
and know that it is there because of you.*

CONOVER SWOFFORD

I have learned from experience that the greater part of our happiness or misery depends on our dispositions and not on our circumstances.

MARTHA WASHINGTON

It is not how many years we live,
but what we do with them.

CATHERINE BOOTH

Is prayer your steering wheel or your spare tire?

CORRIE TEN BOOM

*The God who made your children
will hear your petitions.
After all, He loves them more than you do.*

JAMES DOBSON

Now the God of hope fill you with all joy
and peace in believing, that ye may abound in hope,
through the power of the Holy Ghost.

ROMANS 15:13

We walk without fear,
full of hope and courage
and strength to do His will,
waiting for the endless good
which He is always giving as fast
as He can get us able to take it in.

GEORGE MACDONALD

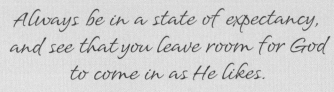

*Always be in a state of expectancy,
and see that you leave room for God
to come in as He likes.*

OSWALD CHAMBERS

It's faith in something and enthusiasm
for something that makes a life worth living.

OLIVER WENDELL HOLMES

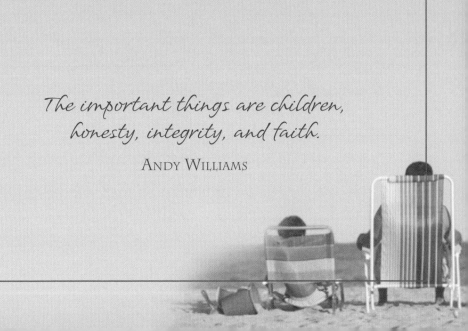

The important things are children, honesty, integrity, and faith.

ANDY WILLIAMS

Therefore choose life, that both thou
and thy seed may live:
that thou mayest love the LORD thy God,
and that thou mayest obey his voice,
and that thou mayest cleave unto him:
for he is thy life, and the length of thy days.

DEUTERONOMY 30:19–20

We need to love our family for who they are
and not for what they do.

KAREN McDUFFY

*A child is like a piece of paper on which
every passerby leaves a mark.*

CHINESE PROVERB

I have learned that success is measured not so much
by the position one has reached in life
as by the obstacles he has overcome.

BOOKER T. WASHINGTON

*It's never too late to be what
you might have been.*

GEORGE ELIOT

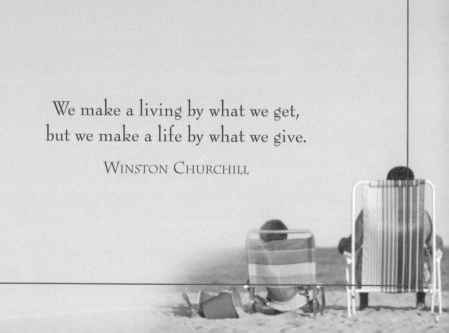

We make a living by what we get,
but we make a life by what we give.

WINSTON CHURCHILL

I have been young, and now am old;
yet have I not seen the righteous forsaken,
nor his seed begging bread.

PSALM 37:25

What do we live for if it is not to make life less difficult for each other?

GEORGE ELIOT

One generation plants the trees;
another gets the shade.

CHINESE PROVERB

Be ye followers of me,
even as I also am of Christ.

1 Corinthians 11:1

Our children are like mirrors reflecting to us whatever attitudes we show them.

CONOVER SWOFFORD

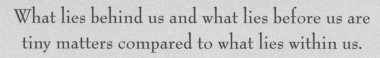

What lies behind us and what lies before us are tiny matters compared to what lies within us.

OLIVER WENDELL HOLMES

I expect to pass through life but once.
If, therefore, there can be any kindness I can show,
or any good things I can do to any fellow human being,
let me do it now and not defer it or neglect it,
as I shall not pass this way again.

WILLIAM PENN

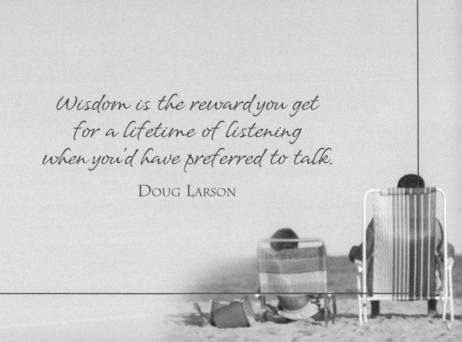

*Wisdom is the reward you get
for a lifetime of listening
when you'd have preferred to talk.*

DOUG LARSON

The fear of the LORD is the beginning of knowledge:
but fools despise wisdom and instruction.

PROVERBS 1:7

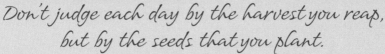

*Don't judge each day by the harvest you reap,
but by the seeds that you plant.*

ROBERT LOUIS STEVENSON

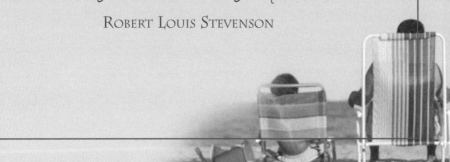

Your family and your love
must be cultivated like a garden.
Time, effort, and imagination
must be summoned constantly
to keep any relationship
flourishing and growing.

JIM ROHN

Perfection, in a Christian sense,
means becoming mature enough
to give ourselves to others.

KATHLEEN NORRIS

How far you go in life depends on
your being tender with the young,
compassionate with the aged,
sympathetic with the striving,
and tolerant of the weak and strong.
Because someday in life
you will have been all of these.

GEORGE WASHINGTON CARVER

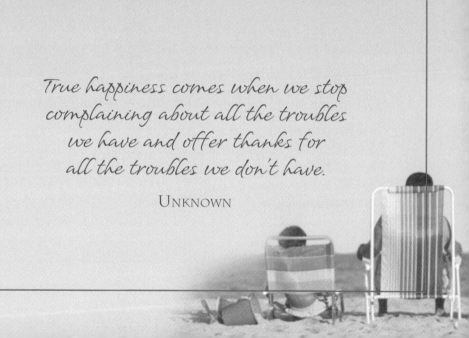

True happiness comes when we stop
complaining about all the troubles
we have and offer thanks for
all the troubles we don't have.

UNKNOWN

When we do the best that we can, we never know
what miracle is wrought in our life,
or in the life of another.

HELEN KELLER

You are never too old to set another goal
or to dream a new dream.

LES BROWN

*It is said that a society can be judged
by the way it treats its children.*

RICHARD N. GOTTFRIED

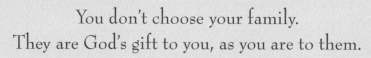

You don't choose your family.
They are God's gift to you, as you are to them.

DESMOND TUTU

One of the secrets of a long and fruitful life
is to forgive everybody everything
every night before you go to bed.

BERNARD M. BARUCH

Children are our most valuable
natural resource.

HERBERT HOOVER

*To waken interest and kindle enthusiasm
is the sure way to teach easily
and successfully.*

TRYON EDWARDS

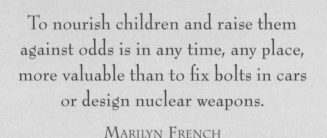

To nourish children and raise them
against odds is in any time, any place,
more valuable than to fix bolts in cars
or design nuclear weapons.

MARILYN FRENCH

Nor need we power or splendor,
wide hall or lordly dome;
the good, the true, the tender—
these form the wealth of home.

Sarah J. Hale

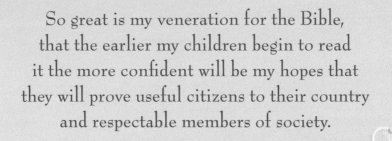

So great is my veneration for the Bible,
that the earlier my children begin to read
it the more confident will be my hopes that
they will prove useful citizens to their country
and respectable members of society.

JOHN QUINCY ADAMS

We don't need more strength
or more ability or greater opportunity.
What we need is to use what we have.

Basil S. Walsh

The secret of happiness is to make others
believe they are the cause of it.

UNKNOWN

*The quality of a person's life
is in direct proportion to their
commitment to excellence,
regardless of their chosen field of endeavor.*

Vince Lombardi

This book of the law shall not depart out of thy mouth;
but thou shalt meditate therein day and night,
that thou mayest observe to do
according to all that is written therein:
for then thou shalt make thy way prosperous,
and then thou shalt have good success.

JOSHUA 1:8